TEARS OF THE

WIDOWS

By

AMB. ELIJAH OBAKA JOHN

AUTHOR'S CONTACTS

Email: ambelijahjohn@gmail.com

Phone: +2348159444983

TABLE OF CONTENTS

INTRODUCTION

As a human rights activist for widows and orphans matters, the issues of TEARS OF THE WIDOWS need our intervention in many communities.

These issues affect our mothers, sisters, Aunts, daughters, wives, and hence the need to address them. Society, individuals, and religious people have to be made aware of these issues and helped as to how they can help and deal with the overwhelming problems affecting women, mostly widows. This will empower them on what to do when they are confronted with a similar problem.

Widowhood is one of the issues that people do not want to talk about. It is a taboo, and you don't speak about the dead. Yet this is an issue that is increasing in our communities because of the number of death occurring. There are many women who have become widows, and some are widowed at an early age. Boko Haram, Fulani Herdsmen, HIV Aids even hunger and hardship has contributed to the number of widows, both young and old, in Nigeria.

How are these women helped to cope with their situation? What role can individuals, communities, and religious people play in helping such women begin to heal?

How can we be equipped to go to the community and bring significant change to many widows who are suffering and have lost hope? How can the understanding of Gender and religious belief help overcome the tears of the widows and their challenges of pain and grief and bring healing to them?

This book is going to look at this neglected area of Concern that needs to be addressed in societies, individuals even in our religion's system. This book will help a widow deal with grief and clean up their tears. This book will help individuals to see the need to support the widows in their time of pain and agony.

This book will empower individuals and communities to treat widows with respect and

help them to go through their grief with dignity
and hope.

CHAPTER *ONE*

COPING WITH THE DEATH OF A SPOUSE

A. The death of a spouse can be one of the most painful events a person ever experiences. The loss of your spouse can mean the loss of your partner, lover, best friend, confidant, and the parent of your children. In addition to dealing with the loss emotionally, a surviving spouse often faces major life changes that can be stressful. Coping with the loss of your spouse involves working through the emotional grief while adjusting to new circumstances.

WHAT TO EXPECT

- **Stages of grief:** Everyone grief differently, but there are some common emotional transitions that are often referred to as the "stages of grief." You may experience some or all of the following:
- **Shock or denial:** One of the first emotions that many people feel is disbelief. You might

feel numb or think, "This isn't possible," or "There has been some kind of mistake." Pretending that something so horrible isn't true sometimes allows a little more time to transition to an unwelcome reality, especially if the loss is unexpected.

- **Anger:** It's common to have feelings of anger. You may be angry at the bearer of bad news or even at your spouse for leaving you. It is also common to be angry at a doctor for being unable to save your spouse or at a higher power for not protecting her. Anger is a normal response to the death of a loved one. It's perfectly understandable to want to try to find out whose fault the loss was and whether it could have been prevented.

- **Bargaining:** In this stage, you might seek to negotiate the return of your spouse no matter how unrealistic these kinds of thoughts may be. For example, some people beg a higher power for more time with their spouse, promising something in exchange. Sometimes this stage is referred to as the "if only." For example, you may think that if only the doctor or you had done something differently, your spouse might have survived.

- **Sadness:** Many people experience deep sadness when the full weight of what has happened sinks in. Suddenly or gradually, you will see that you can't change the situation and will begin to understand what it will mean to go through life without the person you love. You may feel very sad and maybe even guilty about not being there to say goodbye to your spouse or things you wish you had done differently in your relationship.

B. Acceptance. At some point, you will accept your loss and begin to adjust to the new chapter in your life. Memories start making you smile instead of breaking into tears. You might even experience a sense of peace that comes with acceptance.

All of these feelings are normal. However, it is important to remember that there is no set process for grief. Each person's experience is unique. You might find that you skip some of these stages or experience more than one stage at a time, sometimes on the same day.

There isn't a timetable for "getting over" a spouse's death. The pain usually lessens over time, but it may never go away completely. Feelings of mourning may resurface on holidays, on your anniversary, or when you visit a place that was special to the two of you. Seek help if painful feelings don't lessen over time or if they seem more than you can bear. A counselor or therapist can help you to work through this difficult grief process.

Changes

One of the most difficult parts of grieving the loss of a spouse is learning to live with the resulting changes. The transition from being part of a couple to being a single, separate person can be painful and frustrating. You are facing a new set of problems alone instead of handling situations with your spouse. If the loss of your spouse was anticipated, perhaps you already have some plans in place. If the death of your spouse was sudden and unexpected, it might be a while before you become aware of all of the changes that will take place.

It can be frightening when you don't know what to expect or your circumstances suddenly change. You may experience:

- **Financial changes:** Depending on your financial situation, you may have to rework your budget to make ends meet. Some surviving spouses decide to work full-time if they worked part-time or didn't work before. Some look for a more affordable home to meet their financial needs. Evaluate your entire financial situation as well as your emotional state before making any big changes.

- **New location:** Some surviving spouses move for a new job, to be closer to family, or to a home that is more affordable or easier to maintain. A move can be a big change, whether it's within the same community or in another state. Many experts suggest that you try to put off big changes such as a move until you've had a chance to adapt to your new situation. If you decide to move, enlist the help of trusted friends or family members. In addition to helping you with the move itself, they can help you search for a new home and locate important resources (such as mail-forwarding forms or phone service companies in your new area)

C. Learning new skills. It can be overwhelming and confusing to try to take care of everything your spouse is responsible for. You may have to learn to cook, mow the lawn, clean, make repairs, and care for children. Accept or ask for help as you learn how to handle things on your own.

• **Redefining yourself:** You are used to being the most important person in your spouse's life. You're used to living a certain way and sharing favorite activities with your spouse.

Now your identity is changing. You may have to re-establish your goals, values, and priorities in light of your changed circumstances. It is normal to start questioning who you are or what you enjoy in addition to what you used to do because of your spouse's interest and what you did for yourself.

- **Social changes:** Some of your relationships may have been based on the fact that you were a couple. The friends you socialize with as a couple may feel awkward around you as an individual or because they don't know what to say about your spouse's death. Try to focus on relationships that remain supportive. You might even establish a new friendship with someone who has had a similar experience.

- **Parenting changes:** If you have children, you are now experiencing life as a single parent. Lean on your support network as you make this difficult transition. Join a single-parent support group. Other parents may be able to give you ideas and advice on everything from finding backup child care in your area to discipline.

As you begin to piece together a life without your spouse, avoid making big changes too fast. For example, you may want to move immediately because it's too painful to be in the home you shared with your spouse. But this may not be the best option financially. Take your time when making changes and decisions, and get help from friends and family whenever you need it, especially if there are decisions that need to be made right away.

Tips on coping

There's no right way to grieve. Each person's experience is different, and each person copes in his own way. Here are some ideas that can help you cope with your loss:

- **Allow yourself to hurt:** It is important to your healing process that you acknowledge the grief you are experiencing. Let yourself cry if you feel like it. Crying is a healthy way to release emotion and relieve tension. It can also be a way of actively working through your pain. There are no shortcuts; the only way through your grief is to allow yourself to feel the full range of emotions at a pace that feels right to you.

- **Lean on the people you love and who love you:** Grief is often easier to bear when shared with someone. Talk to your close friends or family members about how you are feeling, about your favorite memories with your spouse, and about what you will miss about your spouse. Surround yourself with compassionate people who allow you to grieve in your own way. Avoid confiding in people who try to provide quick fixes for your grief, such as "Just get over it" or "At least you're young enough to marry again." While these people might mean well, they may not know what to say, and their words can be very painful. Instead, choose to spend time with people who are supportive and helpful.

- **Ask for help when you need it:** Chances are your friends and family members want to help, but they may feel awkward because they don't know how to talk with you about your loss, and they aren't sure what they can do to help. Let them know what you need, whether it's someone to listen to or help cook a meal when you just don't have the energy to do it yourself.

- **Move on at your own pace:** Some people may urge you to put your spouse's belongings away or to remove your wedding band. Do these things when you are ready, not on someone else's schedule. No one else shared the same relationship with your spouse. As a result, your grief is entirely unique. Take your time and move through your grief in a way that feels right for you.

- **Consider your spirituality:** You may find it comforting to talk with your spiritual leader or a friend who shares your faith about the role your spirituality is playing in your life and feelings right now.

- Express yourself. Many people find it helpful to write about their feelings in a journal, which can be as effective as talking with someone about them. Write a letter to your spouse to express the things you never shared but wish you had.

Tell your spouse how much she means to you or what you would do differently if you had the chance. This is a great way to express things left unsaid, especially if you didn't get a chance to say goodbye. You may also be able to release pent-up emotions through art or music.

- **Take care of yourself:** Make sure to continue to eat right and to get enough sleep. Also, make an effort to get exercise, even when you don't feel like it. Take a brief walk outside every day if possible. Fresh air, sunlight, and exposure to the natural world can be very calming during a difficult time.

- **Prepare for holidays and other special events:** Even though your grief will lessen, it may resurface from time to time, especially during special holidays. Talk to family members about how traditions might change now that your spouse is gone. You might decide to hold a holiday meal at someone else's home or make a special toast in memory of your spouse.

- **Avoid unhealthy coping strategies:** Alcohol and drugs may seem to help at first, but they may contribute to depressed feelings or just mask the grief and delay the grieving process.

- **Cherish your memories of your spouse:** If there were certain places or events you enjoyed together, Make a photo album or scrapbook of them. If your spouse loved roses, plant a rose bush in his honor. Memorialize your spouse by donating a bench to his favorite park or by starting a scholarship fund in his name if he values education. Supported an organization that was important to him. These actions can help you feel like your spouse's memory will live on and remind you that his life had meaning.

- Talk to a counselor or therapist that can provide additional support and can help you to gain a sense of control and to work through your feelings of grief. Talking to a counselor or therapist can also help you to bring closure to unresolved issues you may have had in your relationship with your spouse. Contact your healthcare provider or the program that sent you this article to locate one in your area.

- **Attend a support group:** Support groups can provide emotional support and can help you understand what to expect after your loss. They also help you see that you are not alone. Other people in a support group will truly understand and sympathize because they have experienced a similar loss. Counselors, spiritual leaders, or healthcare providers in your area might be able to locate a support group near you.

If you have children, you will need to help them to grieve while you are facing the difficult task yourself.

Here are some tips to help:

• Encourage your children to talk about their feelings.

√ Listen to what your children have to say and be supportive.

√ Help them to match words to feelings.

√ Answer any questions they might have; your children may have a lot of questions now and later as they begin to understand death better.

√ Be careful not to overwhelm them with excessive detail, but give simple, basic answers. Be honest in your responses and use words that they will be able to understand.

√ Don't hide your sadness. Show your children that it is okay to express his or her feelings by stating how you feel. Don't, however, vent frustration to them or overburden them with your sadness.

√ Talk to an adult friend or family member when you need to lean on someone.

√ Try to maintain a routine. Routines are very comforting for both children and adults. Keeping up an old routine can help your children to feel secure when so many things are changing. Continue to eat dinner together, follow the same bedtime routine, and maintain the same general schedule you followed before your spouse's death. If you need help driving your children places, cooking dinner, or with anything else, ask a close friend or relative to lend a hand.

√ Let your child's teachers know what has happened. They can be alert for signs that your child needs help coping and provide extra support during this difficult time.

√ Show your children that you are still there to take care of them. After losing one parent, your children may fear losing you. Spend time with your children and provide reassurance.

Younger children may need extra cuddling from you to feel secure.

√ Understand that children have unique ways of grieving, too. Older children may retreat or not want to talk about their parents because it's too painful. Younger children may not fully understand what has happened or need extra love and support. Children can experience the same grief stages as adults, so watch your children carefully to see what they need from you and others right now and in the future.

You may also want to consider getting professional help for your children. Losing a parent can be a traumatic event for a child of any age. A professional counselor can help your children learn ways to cope with this enormous loss.

LOOKING FORWARD

You will probably never stop missing your spouse, but that doesn't mean that you can't go on to live a fulfilling life. While your future might look different than you originally anticipated, it can still be enjoyable, interesting, and exciting. It may seem hard to believe at first, but SOMEDAY you will be able to tell someone else that there is hope, that you will survive, and that life does go on.

CHAPTER *TWO*

AGONY OF WIDOWHOOD

When women get married, they enter it with the blissful thoughts of a wonderful life with their husbands for the rest of their lives. But it is hard to accept the reality that when they walk into marriage, they are all potential widows.

When a woman loses her husband, she must be forced to face the reality of mortality and how to move on and create a new life for herself and her children.

<u>MY EXPERIENCE AS A WIDOW'S MINISTER.</u>

As I have grappled with the various challenges that have come to some widows way, I have worked closely with many widows, and I have watched their journey, sometimes in sadness and sometimes in joy.

With all I learned, the idea of writing a book was born inside of me.

However, being a very busy father with my family and handling various responsibilities, I hardly had the time to put pen to paper. But thank God for this time.

So what did I want to share out? What wisdom could I possibly impart in this book? I want to share all I experienced in my journey with the widows and those who were about to step into the reality of life or were already living it.

√ I want to touch the single man and woman who is about to or is newly married, the married man and woman, the new widow still grappling with grief, and the old widow who has managed to find a 'new normal.'

√ I want to cry out to them with a voice of hope that their life is not yet over and the fact that they are still here means that they have a purpose of fulfilling and they can go on to live a full life.

√ I want to share with them how to tackle all the challenges they are facing. How I know that the loss of a loved one does not end there, for many have gone on to face the loss of family, friends, children, and even their place in society.

A widow is thrown into an emotional whirlwind, and it is only with the right kind of support for those around her that she is able to pick herself up and find healing.

Support is a must for widows, and it is by leaning against this backbone that she is able to make it.

One of the first challenges widows face is realizing that the fact that their husbands had not written a will would keep them in court.

This is a real tragedy. In the beginning, some had little knowledge of what the law meant for them, and they were forced to learn this painfully after the death of their husbands.

It made me wonder how many potential widows out there are about to be embroiled in legal battles, all because they did not know the law and how it could protect them and their children.

√ I want to let them know that it is important for them and their husbands to write up a comprehensive will and to stress that they need to understand family law and how it affects and applies to them.

I desired to let people know what I had come to learn as a minister to the widows.

The struggles a widow is likely to face are a result of the areas of her marriage that were not correctly structured.

The right foundation in marriage is critical for the fulfillment of the couple but also the protection of the family that you are building together.

One of the lessons I felt is vital to share the fact that as a new widow, you cannot afford to let go of the reins of your life as you grapple with your grief.

I want you to learn that there are some who will use such an opportunity to take advantage of the grieving widow and her family.

Women have to stand up and own their lives, whether they are married or not.

George Washington Carver said: *"Where there is no vision, there is no hope."*

In addition, I would stress that a woman should build her financial knowledge and focus on building an inheritance for her children.

Another paramount issue I would point out is the come-we-stay relationships that are very common in our society today, mostly in Nigeria.

I would caution and advise women in such a union to push for it to be legalized.

There are many women who face complications and suffer at the hands of other women their husbands may have been involved with or with in-laws who did not recognize their union. Women should understand that they can have a hand in ensuring a better future for themselves and their children, no matter what befalls them.

PAINS THAT WIDOWS GO THROUGH AFTER THE DEATH OF THEIR HUSBAND

The pains that some women go through after the death of their spouses are horrific

Women have remained an economically disenfranchised lot in Nigeria for far too long. The inability of most of them to own property, especially land and housing, has continued to perpetuate their economic dependence on their husbands.

Consequently, women become extremely vulnerable upon a husband's death, with the lives of many being turned into a living hell, not just by their in-laws but also the society in general.

Because theirs is a dog's life, widows see it all. Some are blamed for the demise of their husbands, especially when the deaths are mysterious or as a result of suicide or murder. Others get disowned and chased away by in-laws upon the death of their husbands.

Needless to say, those who get embroiled in nasty court battles over property or those who get forced to participate in backward cultural practices like widow cleansing and wife inheritance. Others have to engage themselves in high-risk work to make ends meet following abandonment by in-laws.

Need we state that some have to constantly fight stigma from society, especially from their married counterparts who treat them with the suspicion that they can steal their husbands?

Some years ago, a widow from Benue state in Nigeria lost millions worth of property to her stepsons. So nasty were wrangles between her and her two stepsons that involved the court.

Unfortunately for her, she lost the bid to inherit the property she had been eyeing for over 11 years after the court ruled in her step sons' favor.

Her stepson's line of argument was that the disputed property did not belong to their late father but to their late mother.

One of the widows told me besides the challenge of being romantically involved with a new lover without being judged harshly by her in-laws and society, widowhood has strengthened her, she says.

"Her husband was key in making decisions affecting the family. She suddenly had to do this alone, and she has slowly learned to take on challenges as they come," says the woman, who, after losing her husband to HIV/aids, was chased away from her home by in-laws who blamed her for her husband's death.

She had to go and live with a friendly distant relative with her children. The stressful life, she said, has seen her health rapidly deteriorate.

Never mind, this is happening in a country where, on paper, the laws recognize women's rights, but in practice, many widows are chased away from their land, and access to justice is hard to obtain.

In the villages, she says, courts are distant whilst ties between blood relatives are very strong; suing them will put one in awkward situations.

Hear her: "Again, most widows can't afford court cases. If anything, they are time-consuming and are culturally frowned upon for family disputes. Going to court worsens the relationship between widows and in-laws. How do you go back to such a home after winning a case against them?"

Many others that she said to me were of strained relationships with their in-laws after the death of their husbands. One common prayer and hope they all seemed to have is for government and non-government organizations to set up a support program to protect and look into the welfare of widows.

Widow's disproportionate exclusion from property ownership is a common feature in this country. It's time for government, civil society, and religious bodies to make deliberate efforts to protect widows from discriminatory customs enshrined in patriarchy, religious laws, and institutional practices that severely restrict the ability to gain and control such property.

In some parts of Africa, widow cleansing and inheritance are still observed as cultural aspect. According to traditions among African countries, for instance, widows are expected to engage in sexual intercourse with a "cleanser," who may be a family member or a 'professional cleanser' who gets hired specifically for that purpose.

"This is done in order to rid the widow of impurity ascribed to her after her husband's death," says Kate, an elderly widow from one of the community.

The elder says, seeing as couples in a tradition whose practice despite being in sharp decline, is still actively practiced in rural outposts — are traditionally expected to engage in sex preceding specific activities like planting, building homes, and other significant cultural and social events, widows are always expected to be cleansed before taking part in such activities, and that is how "professional cleansers" come in.

Anything short of this, he says, they won't be allowed to participate lest they invite the wrath of their ancestors upon their clan and in-laws.

For most of these widows, their life is a delicate balancing act, getting infected with deadly sexually transmitted diseases such as HIV/aids and meeting cultural expectations.

"In rural outposts, sexual abstinence tends to undermine cultural expectations in widowhood. What's more, the use of condoms is never allowed when fulfilling culturally prescribed sexual rituals.

"Never mind, most of these widows are vulnerable and can't negotiate for safer sex," says Ali, a health worker based in Bornu and a part-time nursing tutor in the area.

"Widow Inheritance is, however, now getting frowned upon because there are enough reports that show it is partly responsible for the high prevalence of HIV in the area," says Kate, who acknowledges that the region has the highest HIV prevalence in the country.

CHAPTER *THREE*

DEATH OF A HUSBAND AND THE ROLE OF THE CHURCH

Each type of loss brings its own kind of pain, challenges, reactions, and responses.

The death of a husband is a painful experience, especially tragic death.

It leaves the wife devastated, confused, and without hope.

Mr. Peter confirms this in the following observations: *"Loss of a wife or a husband is much more difficult. Burdens that previously were shared must now be borne alone, and that can be very stressful."*

Immediately the wife is called a widow; her plans and future are doomed. In our African society, the dignity she had is stripped. The woman is made vulnerable and feels marginalized, with very few to turn to for support.

Mr. Godwin has remarked concerning African Practices that: *"The death of a husband heralds a period of imprisonment and hostility to the wife or wives. This treatment may or may not be out of malice, but in all cases, women suffer and are subjected to rituals that are health hazards and heart-rending,"* It is a difficult time indeed when she is confronted with questions, Why me God? Why are they treating me like this? Do they think I killed my husband? How should I continue with life from here? Who should I turn to, someone who will be able to understand what I am going through? With these and many more unanswered questions, she has to make major decisions about her life and that of her children.

News of the death of a husband will come as a shock to many women, mostly if it is through tragic accidents and or that of young husbands. One young widow shared with me how she could not believe the news broken to her by the police of the car accident that killed her husband. She thought for a moment that they were lying to her that it could not be her husband. She said, "You have taken my husband alive to the mortuary. I will not believe you unless I feel him." The way Mrs. Margaret Audu relates the story of the death of her husband at one of our widow's conferences on June 23, 2015.

The news of a husband's death breaks too many women and is very insensitive, and leaves them in a state of shock without someone close to turning to for support. Sometimes people are not sensitive enough to how much this can affect the person's life.

Our African communities are supposed to be supportive but are confronted with "cultural practices," which often leave the widow victimized and a victim. Many people no longer live in family units or clans that can support them at a time like this. The husband may die whilst both of you are away working in the urban area, and your immediate family members are far.

A widow explains;

"I lost my husband in 2009 as a result of Boko Haram killing in Yobe state. I had gone through a lot of trauma to get all this into perspective. It was very difficult for me because this happened in Yobe, the northern part of Nigeria when I was so far away from my family in the East part of Nigeria. My husband was killed by unknown gunmen on that faithful Friday morning, and I only got to know about it on a Tuesday morning in the following week. I will not forget that terrible week when I had to plan everything to take his remains back to the East. Since then, it has not been easy; I miss him and often feel lonely.

Whenever I needed comfort or support from my fellow women, even Christian women, I was repeatedly told that I was not alone. They tried to point out to me that I am now married to God by quoting from Isaiah 54: 4-5 "Do not be afraid; you will not suffer shame. Do not fear disgrace; you will not be humiliated. You will forget the shame of your youth and remember no more the reproach of your widowhood. For your Maker is, your husband- the Lord God Almighty is his name."

They further said that Jesus Christ was going to be the father of my children and that I should ask him for anything. When a person is made vulnerable, one has no choice but to listen."

Practically speaking, what these Christian women think and say is not possible in real life. They assume that God becomes the husband of only the widows. What about the single women and the married women too, *"Is God not also there for them?*

There are times when one is lonely and needs someone to talk to just to air out what is in your heart. In this case, a physical presence of a person who you can just hug and make you feel not abandoned is more applicable.

I do not deny the fact that the presence of God is always with the widows and in their children, but there are times one remembers the role the husband played and misses that. Many times the Bible is misinterpreted, making innocent people become more vulnerable.

Church people will not quote the passages in the Bible that empower widows and that gives the Church responsibility to look after them. Places like James 1:27 say, *"Pure religion and undefiled before God and the Father is this, to visit the fatherless and widows in their affliction, and to keep himself unspotted from the world."* You see, I am mindful that many of my mothers, aunties, and sisters who are widows are going through hard experiences and are not able to speak out and have no one to turn to for solidarity.

HARMFUL CULTURAL PRACTICES.

Cultural practices differ from one ethnic grouping to another and from one family clan to another. There are many customs and practices that people follow when death occurs in a family. More of these customs and practices are expected and targeted to be observed by a widow. The woman is seen at this time as not being in a position to make concrete decisions. Decisions are on her. She cannot decide on how her husband's funeral should be. Of course, someone said, and I quote: *"Grief usually involves intense sorrow, pain, loneliness, anger, depression, physical symptoms, and changes in interpersonal relationships."*

But this should not make the family take things for granted, that the widow is not in a position to make her own decisions. The family even decides who has to inherit the property without her consent. She is made vulnerable and expected to go through all the customs/traditions, and rituals without question.

One Mrs. Margaret was accused of not crying loudly for everybody to notice that she was the widow. This case may suggest that people do not come to comfort you at a difficult time, but they come to see and witness the way you are handling your grief and then talk about it behind your back.

Some of the harmful practices are:

Widowhood Cleansing

The concept of ritual cleansing is rooted in many traditional societies in Africa, mostly Nigeria.

Rituals are performed after the death to cleanse or purify the affected person and, in this case, the widow. They do this in fear of evil spirits that are regarded as agents of death. A widow, in this case, is regarded as being ritually unclean because of her husband's death. She goes through many hazardous experiences.

Even though the Government of Nigeria is trying to educate communities through their traditional Authorities on the dangers of practicing such rituals because of HIV Aids, some families continue to practice cleansing rituals.

These are members that belong to Churches and other religions, hence the need for Churches to take a leading role in helping to raise awareness of the dangers of these practices. Those that still practice feel that mourning the deceased is complete when the wife performs the required rituals. The most common

The cleansing ritual is what they call "Taking away death." In this practice, a man is identified in the community to perform the ritual of cleansing and is paid. His responsibility is to have sexual intercourse with the widow. In doing this, the family believes that they are cleansed from evil spirits that cause death. But this raises many questions. What has sexual intercourse got to do with the cleansing of the whole family clan? Why should it be the poor woman who is already suffering because of the death of her husband made to suffer more?

There is no respect for this woman who once was the wife of their son; they cannot give her the dignity she requires and deserves. She does not just lose a husband; she also loses her integrity, identity, dignity, and her property, which could sustain her and the children. The woman is not consulted on what will happen so that she can give consent to what will happen and maybe have a choice of a man. In many cases, they say the man asked to do this kind of job could be someone who is mentally not well, a dirty, unclean man. Why? What have the government and religious bodies said about this? Young widows have a problem because they have no one to turn to for support because the older people would want to make sure that they go through what they did. This experience is not only in Nigeria but in most of Africa.

The example of a young widow In Kenya who received advice from an older widow who claimed to be born–again Christian saying, **"Don't follow Christianity blindly."** When it comes to tradition, make sure that you put your house in order. When she asked what she meant by that, the old widow said you pull down your pants. It is the way things are done, it will only be for one night, and your family will be taken care of. In the morning, you can repent and go on with your Christianity. Women have suffered this silently, and other women have forced them to go through the experiences they had.

In the context of HIV Aids, what would be the outcome? There are two possible scenarios, either the woman may infect the man if she is positive, or the man, because of doing this kind of ceremony too many women, may be positive and infect the innocent woman with HIV or STIs.

INHERITANCE

A widow may be inherited by her in-laws so that they can control the property and children. Where there is no inheritance, the in-laws make sure that all the property is taken away from her, and left with nothing – she has to raise children on her own without support. In places where the Church has played a role in

Stopping widowhood rituals, the African Christian widow still remains handicapped in terms of finance and property inheritance. If the widow is not doing anything or is in paid employment, she is thrown into penury, which goes against her.

Some women suffer after many years of working in the home and having acquired property together with their husbands; all are taken away, and they are left with children without money to survive.

Mrs. Gloria Idoko was lucky in this case because the husband told his relatives before he died that most of the property they had was bought by the wife. For this reason, they told her that all the property belonged to her. After taking all the property, the woman is left with children, and she has to dress in black or white to show that she is mourning her husband. The mourning period varies from family to family, but many times this takes at least period of seven to nine months.

Isolation from the real world Many widows had expressed that the most torturing experience they went through was when they were left alone with no one to talk to.

Remember that she has no choice of clothes. She is expected to wear black or white during this mourning period as she is not supposed to wear fancy clothes. Black or white is a sign of mourning. Some traditions shave the hair of the widow so that she does not have to style the hair.

Older women put on a blackhead scarf all the time. She is a different person with a different appearance. Left alone, what will be in her mind? She cannot eat with others and uses old plates, which will be destroyed after the ritual is done. She is restricted socially. She is not allowed to visit other homes or shake hands with people.

At a time when she needs support and comfort to help her begin to get to terms with what has happened, she is made to be alone – lonely with no one to talk to, which in many cases affects her physical health. To be silent and not seen talking is one of the virtues of a good grieving widow – so is believed and taught. She is marginalized and without decisions to make, only following the dictates of her in-laws.

Many women suffer silently and become lonely, which leads to depression. This has resulted in some women dying early thereafter because of such treatment. Now as a single person, the widow begins to experience what single women go through. She must not speak to men; otherwise, she will entice them.

As much as someone may want to help and assist the widow, he may find it difficult because of what people will say. It is as if all the men become her relations. She is afraid of how to address certain issues; she will need someone to be with her as a witness. In the professional world, it is difficult because you cannot work with women only. It is also difficult for a person to always ask someone to accompany you if you will be meeting with men. A stigma is attached to widowhood.

Impact on children.

Children grow to see the negative treatment that their mother gets from her relatives, and this affects them psychologically. Many children have not done well at school, dropped out of school, and have grown up miserable. Other children, when they grow up, have applied such negative treatment to their wives when they marry because they think that is how women should be treated. So, you can see that the treatment that the mother gets, children see to be abnormal, and it reflects on their future life. Some of the children that we see in the streets today or as drug addicts are the result of the treatment they went through after the death of their father.

WHY IS THIS A RELIGIOUS ISSUE?

Widowhood is a religious issue because it deals with human dignity. We need to look at our religions and see what we can do to address the issue. What does God say about widows? How can dignity be restored to these women when they read the scriptures? Will they find affirmation? What is the role of the Christian Church on issues of maltreatment of the widows?

These are some of the questions that we need to look at and address so that dignity is restored and healing is achieved. Many women become widows at an early stage, a difficult time of uncertainty and reproach. This needs some mechanisms or special facilities that would help and assist them in healing and liberating themselves from unfortunate and negative widowhood experiences.

Unlike the white community, they have counseling facilities, and immediately, they are able to see a family doctor and or a psychologist. In many cases, a will is made, and the community accepts it when the widow decides to remarry. On the contrary, in our African society, this is not the case; as said earlier, the widow is expected to go through painful experiences adding on top of the pain she has already of losing her dear husband. The widow is expected to go through all mourning rites in order to be accepted again in the community. As Mr. Olayinka puts it: "It is assumed that a husband's soul will not rest until the widow has completed elaborate mourning rites and has been purified."

I conducted a Widows program in December 2014 with women who are widows within the community of Niger State. The experiences of these women were very traumatic; they had never had a chance to talk about their experiences of widowhood. Some of them had been widowed for more than ten years and still hoped that one day their husband would return. They were afraid to sleep alone in the bedroom because of all the nightmares they had.

Some would sleep with the door open, thinking that the husband would come whilst they were asleep and should not miss the door that leads to his former bedroom. How can these women be helped to understand death and to go through the grieving stages, which will help them accept it as they have to move on with life?

What mechanisms or systems are there in the Church or other religions put in place to help and assist widows in their experience of pain as well as their healing? How do widows understand the liberation wrought by a God who was so particular about widows and their problems? The community has helped widows to a certain extent, and this kind of support is declining. How can the Church learn from the community, from the support family units give?

Mrs. Salome justifies the need to do theology from such experiences of women and says that: *"Women experience the injustice of being blamed for whatever does not go right. The injustice of having to implement decisions they did not help to make, the injustice of having to struggle to have one's humanity recognized and treated as such, all this becomes the context of struggle reflected in women's theology."*

It is the Church's responsibility to liberate women from the unjust experiences they go through in the community so that their dignity can prevail. Liberation must be viewed as men and women walking together on the journey home, with the Church as the umbrella of faith, hope, and love.

Through some practical Pastoral care models, the Church may achieve wholeness, healing, and liberation for widows and become an instrument of justice for widows and those who are marginalized. The Church is asked to be in solidarity with women because, in the body of Christ, the women members (widows) are in pain.

This raises many challenges for African Churches. The Church should have a properly organized counseling session in which the widow is helped to appraise herself in her new situation realistically. She should be equipped with new skills to avoid disappointments. She will need help to acquire strategies for handling grief without getting hopelessly broken; She should be helped on how to handle loneliness, how to make decisions, and how to cope with her new responsibility as a breadwinner. The Church and its theology should provide refuge and emotional support, acknowledging that the widows are persons created in the image of God.

As Mrs. Salome rightly says:

"The stories we tell of our hurts and joys are sacred. Telling them makes us vulnerable, but without sharing, we cannot build community and solidarity. Our stories are precious paths on which we have walked with God and struggled for a passage to full humanity. They are events through which we have received the blessings of life from the hand of God. I have shared my experiences which have helped me in the healing process".

This is an onward going process. What are the other stories of women we know? The women we worship with, those who have accepted to take leadership positions in our Churches, and yet they have this as a problem, and those women who are our neighbors and belong to the same women's group. Have they been able to share or tell their stories? Have we taken the time to know what they went through? What have they experienced, and what practical pastoral mechanisms have the churches they belong to put in place to help such women go through their experiences with hope? This is our challenge in the teaching of theology.

I urge the Churches to wake up and take responsibility for the pains the widows go through after the death of their husbands.

CHAPTER *FOUR*

WIDOWS MALTREATMENT.

This chapter of the book is birthed by my emotional feelings while interviewing so of the widows around me. The maltreatment of widows used to be worse in the time past, but it could be better than it is now: What widows go through in spite of the influence of religion and Western culture.

It was not uncommon, then, to force a widow to drink the water used in washing her husband's corpse, to prove that she was not responsible for his death, or to force a widow to marry one of her late husband's siblings. While some of these are on the decline or discarded altogether, widows still have unpleasant tales to tell.

One of my experiences was that of a very young lady Mrs. Eunice Frank, a member of the Church where I pastor. My senior pastor and I received a phone call from her friend around 1:45 am that her husband was seriously sick.

Getting there, we met the man at the point of death, and we quickly called on his younger brother to come; after some minutes, the younger brother arrived, and he finally died. Surprisingly, before he was to be taken to the mortuary, the younger brother removed his SIM card from his phone and slotted it in his own. He started maltreating the woman even before they went for the funeral; the company where Mr. Frank worked sent money to the wife and children for the funeral, but the younger puckered the whole money without giving the wife anything.

After the funeral, the company called the wife and brother of Mr. Frank and paid another money to the wife, but the brother-in-law collected the money from her; she was left with no choice but to relocate back to the village with her children. But thank God for the rule of the Church over the young widow's life, we were able to care for her and her two children before she eventually got over the pains, and now she's happily married to another man.

What about Mrs. Roseline, who went on the street begging after she lost her husband many years ago? The day the news of her husband's death came to her, her hopes evaporated. That was when she knew that there was no help from anywhere except God. She was downcast to the extent that she no longer knew what was happening around her. It was as if the whole world had forgotten her.

Before the husband's death, life was very rosy; they were one big family. She realized it was good to be married. Her seven children were happy that they had wonderful parents. She remembered that my husband used to organize regular get-togethers in the house just to get his immediate family closer to his relatives.

All these went through until the day death took him away. Then, she realized how life could be so cruel to a woman whose hope and joy have been taken away. Those who called themselves her husband's relations turned their backs on her. They called her all manner of names, saying that her plan was to inherit the husband's property without giving him a male child. She had seven children, one male, and six female, yet they were not satisfied.

She was shocked at their action. She never believed she could be subjected to such maltreatment from the so-called in-laws and people that never ceased to come to the house while the husband was alive.

Since the death of her husband, his relations do not bother about seven children. They claimed there was no money to send the children to school. All efforts to convince them proved abortive, and she had to take up the challenge of training them. None of them was ready to take care of her and the children.

To worsen the situation, the company that employed her as a cleaner on the contract didn't deem it fit to pay her. As a casual workers, the man in charge of our department keeps giving them different excuses for not paying their wages. She was living on no payment from that company for many months. The man in charge of her department maintains that the company doesn't pay him on a monthly basis; that everything depends on the company.

She has had the course to go on the street begging so that my children can feed and go to school. At times, she weeps over the death of her husband, and her children regularly recall unforgettable moments with their father. Widowhood is not a disease, but it's a painful experience.

Thank God today, Mrs. Roseline's children are all doing better now, under the sponsorship of An NGO. The mystery behind this is God has been faithful. She had always believed that God was the husband of the widow, so when everybody turned their back on her, she trusted in God. And God has been sending good Samaritans to her.

It's a pity that the country in which we live doesn't appreciate the essence of a widow or what she passes through. Society should come and help the widows; many of them are without help, and we are at the mercy of their in-laws who never believe in them. A woman who has no husband, no matter how rich she is, still needs assistance. I don't expect anyone to look down on widows or the fatherless because it can happen to anybody. Death is inevitable.

What about another woman whose husband's relations denied her of her rights? The death of her husband was a mystery. She lost him about five years ago. He was on his way to his business place when a call came that he had been shot by unknown gunmen. The truth is that it wasn't too long before he left the house that the news of his death was brought to her. She was shocked, and for a couple of months, she wasn't myself.

Shockingly, his relatives started threatening her, asking her to quit the house or alternatively marry his younger brother. At that point, she was devastated; she didn't know what to do. There were a series of family meetings concerning that, but she refused the proposal.

She never knew that; that was the beginning of the problem. She started living a life of a frustrated widow. There was no place to go. That was when she knew my husband was dead. His relatives made her go through hell. Today, they have all rejected and promised not to have anything to do with her.

They have denied her all her rights and promised not to cater for their late brother's child. Now, this should teach men who are living with their families a lesson. It's time to make's plans for your family, write your will and make it legal for the protection of your wife and your children; death is inevitable.

I'm at the mercy of my in-laws.

Her marriage lasted more than seventeen years until death came and took her husband away. His relations were against the marriage, but her husband insisted.

For them, it wasn't a wise decision to marry a girl from her hometown, southwest. But he insisted, and they got married. Things were going smoothly for them until some years ago, when he started complaining of stomach aches and died.

"Surprisingly, they didn't attend his funeral, and all of a sudden, they demanded all her husband's landed documents. They didn't bother helping her children. She has three children, and they have squandered his property. They threw her and the children out. Right now, she has no help except God.

A lesson for married women, they should stop living only on their husband's income and create their own way of income so that they can have what to fall back to if unexpected things happen.

It is a pity that people don't see the reason why they have to cater to this particular individual. Another challenge is that some of these widows lack good healthcare facilities.

I am using this book to encourage every well-to-do individual to try and reach out to as many widows as possible so as to be able to mold their lives back to normal. The fact is that Nigerians don't care about their widows, especially as they are exposed to a series of maltreatment and torments by their in-laws.

These people need to be educated because the majority of them are maltreated because of their ignorance.

CHAPTER *FIVE*

HOW TO STAND STRONG AS A WIDOW

Becoming a widow is not an easy thing to handle, but people can survive the tragedy. Here is how widows can cope with the problems they now face. There has been much written about single parents in recent years. But what does it take to survive as a widow who is not a single parent by choice but by the cruel hands of fate?

There are so many widows in Africa, some who are younger than the norm and face a set of challenges all their own. These challenges include a lack of money to feed themselves and their children, unexpected medical bills, the permanent loss of a loved one, and radical shifts in daily routines.

Some young widows can cope without a spouse. Here are some ways widows can survive in the new world they've found themselves in when help is hard to find.

√ LEARN TO LOVE THE LONELINESS

Part of being a widow is learning to spend time alone. But people don't like to be alone, research has suggested. So, how can widows use loneliness to survive?

Well, being alone is something that people can get used to. According to The Huffington Post's Alena Hall, people, no matter if they're an introvert or an extrovert, can learn to accept loneliness and love it.

This is because loneliness has been linked to deepening other relationships, finding new hobbies, and changing scenery. It makes people develop new skills and abilities they may not have considered before the event occurred.

√ LOOK FORWARD TO SEEING YOUR LOST ONE AGAIN

Juliana Adamu didn't know what it meant to be a widow until her husband, Adamu, died. It was then that she sought advice on how to cope, and she shared her experience in the piece; she explained that thinking about the ways in which she would be reminded of her late husband or see him again in the afterlife helped her cope.

"As much as we were a happy family, I always looked forward to being alone with Adamu again," she explained. *"I used to tell the children: 'Listen, sweeties, I married your father, not you, and I look forward to having him all to myself."*

√ HAVE PATIENCE WHEN PEOPLE FORGET YOUR LOST HUSBAND

An important part of being a widow is not getting too upset when someone briefly forgets about the person you lost. Someone once said a speaker and award-winning author wrote an article that explained how often families and friends will forget about the loved one you lost and not be there to help you cope.

The best medicine for a widow in that scenario is not to push those relationships away but to accept that some people aren't going to be there for you all the time, he wrote.

"Part of your transitioning into a life post-loss includes dealing with relationships that may be in flux, evolving or perhaps even disappearing altogether."

√ TAKE CONTROL OF YOUR LIFE

It might seem easy to accept loss and wallow in despair. But that won't help you move on.

As Cicillia noted in an article, widows should prepare to accept the life they're living, take it by the horns, and move on from the darkness when a loved one passes away. That's the only way they can fully embrace the new world they've found themselves in.

Consider getting into good physical shape with an improved diet and a schedule for training.

√ JOIN A COMMUNITY OF PEOPLE WITH SIMILAR EXPERIENCES

As mentioned earlier in this story, there are millions of widows across the country — and they're surely going through similar pains and problems.

One way to survive widowhood is to join a widow network. Some of these networks include Elijah's Widows and Orphans Int'l, which offers resources and information for widows, and The African Widow Project, a social media network for widows. Young widows even have their own social networking sites.

Individual Investors offer advice to widows on improving their financial situations once their loved one passes away. Because financial planning at this stage involves both a person's emotional state and financial state, many widows are pushed by well-meaning relatives and even advisors to make unwise decisions or to make changes before they are ready to do so.

√ GO THROUGH THE PAIN

A new study found that widows tend to get through chronic or physical pain better than those who are married, according to Time magazine. In large part, this is because widows have to go through emotional pain for an extended period of time and are used to enduring the feeling more than a married couple might be, Francine Russo wrote for Time.

This pushes the widow to accept the pain as her own and not rely on others to remedy the situation.

√ TAKE CARE OF YOUR HEALTH

Taking care of your wellness is an important part of being a widow. Weight loss is more harmful to widows than newly married couples because it may start an ongoing weight loss trend. Part of this is connected to how widows may be elderly, and weight loss for the elderly can sometimes be fatal, the study found.

This is a big concern for population health as significant weight loss increases mortality risk, especially among elderly widows. We were especially concerned to see that weight loss following widowhood is significantly greater for African-Americans than for whites.

√ UNDERSTAND THAT YOU CAN LOVE AGAIN

It is possible to love again. Psychology Today's Aaron Ben-Zeev wrote that widows often seek someone new to love once enough time has gone by — which isn't necessarily a bad thing. Being with someone new can help people cope and learn to rebuild relationships, Ben-Zeev wrote, which is crucial for widows to move on from the person they lost.

A young widow can profoundly fall in love, but their loving relationship might be complex as it is typically a three-heart relationship; just as such a relationship is possible when all three hearts are still beating, it is possible in this case as well.

√ ACCEPT THE GRIEVING PROCESS

It's not always easy being a widow, mostly in African countries. You lose your loved one out of the blue, and now you've got to move on with the world.

But a relationship expert wrote on her blog that widows should learn to laugh the pain away and embrace the emotions that come. Bottling up difficult feelings will only cause more pain and torment. Letting emotions out will lead to greener pastures.

www.ingramcontent.com/pod-product-compliance
Lightning Source LLC
Chambersburg PA
CBHW071054260726
48661CB00006B/2279